Secondary Sources

Secondary Sources

Poems by

Mikel Vause

Cover design by Shay Culligan:

ISBN: 978-1-950462-99-5

Kelsay Books Inc.

kelsaybooks.com

**502 S 1040 E, A119
American Fork, Utah 84003**

Many of the poems herein have appeared in various journals including *Weber: The Contemporary West* and *Clover: A Literary Rage.*

Introduction

Life is about experience, mystery, seeking and finding, or, sometimes getting lost. Yet humans still want to peer over the edge, visit dark places on maps, test themselves. Some seek isolation. Others seek spiritual or physical fulfillment. Regardless of motive, there seems to be something innate that draws humans out of their caves into harsh sun or freezing snow. Wilfrid Noyce claims "it's in our nature to go out." That doesn't mean every foray has to be death defying or with a particular purpose, something superhuman. For many, answers can be found sitting under an apple tree, or beside a brook, in one's back garden. The point is those who choose to explore are left to rely on *Secondary Sources*.

Many thanks to family and friends.

Contents

A Most Terrible and Deadly Season

I feel strong for the battle, but I know every ounce of strength will be wanted.
—Base Camp 1924, George Leigh Mallory

Everest is a matter of universal of human endeavor, a cause from which
there is no withdrawal, whatever loses it may demand.
—G.O. Dyrenfurth

It's human to go out
Since the beginning of days
To leave casual collective comfort,
Escape the jail-house of society
Explore on the fringes of existence—
(both physical and metaphysical),
Touch the dark spots on the map
Search for freshness
investigate lost innocents
Lean against the wind
Scratch the surface of iron-hard ice
Taunt tendons, cramped muscle
Grasp cold rock—dig for razor-sharp flakes
War once fulfilled instinctual urge
Price was high
Shackleton fought a war of adventure
Armed only with physical toughness
And creativity
No mortars or Mustard Gas
Only cold isolation
And open water in a small boat
Standard then was set
What was said about history repeating itself
The gauntlet was thrown
On Everest in 1996—It was
A most terrible and deadly season.

Shooting Star

100 yards off the oil and gravel
Of State Road 89
Stands the skeleton
Of hope gone south
Walls of weather-beaten pine
Lists to the west
Pulled closer to horizontal
With each sunset

Broken windows
Mostly missing roof
Allows Sparrows and Jays
Access 24 hours a day

With each step
Burnished leaves
Yellow brown some brittle red
Dry crunch
Echoes bounce and weave
Off gray walls
Push aside dust and clutter
Elbows past tattered old coats
Patched and faded
On hooks or hangers
By the back door
On the floor in heaps
Worn to rags

Dusty memories
Swirl & dance to cosmic music
Sunlight sneaks through chinks
In mud log walls
70 years abandoned
Assails darkness locked
So long in place
Explodes like shooting star.

Gogarty's Pub

Twilight then darkness
Sun retreats to the other side of the world
Dancers swing jump down cobblestone roads
Closed to cars
Past pubs chippeys closed shops
Both young and old
Follow a well-worn path

Live music laughter clinking pints
Pulled together old men lean
Elbows on the bar
Feet push against brass foot rails
Confide with whispers
To neighbors left and right

From worn wooden benches
Rises the low moan of the pipes
Then harmony as old as Time
"Rocky Road to Dublin 1 2 3 4 5"
Takes control of hearts and minds

Hidden behind smoke laughter
Wreathed in music
Irish pipes mandolin banjo
Pounding rhythm of bodhran
Clapping hands feet tapping punctuate

Sad Cloudy eyes stare at a pint of Guinness
Gripped in gnarled knotted fingers of rough hands
That know what it is to cut peat thresh barley
Clear rocky ground by hand
Build dry stone walls

Rough tweeds of Irish wool
Musty from never being completely dry
Hang on sloped shoulders
Flat cap rests cockeyed on wispy gray hair

Deep furrows cut down stubbled cheeks
Still silent as a dead man
Lifts pint to cracked chapped lips
Slight smile turns mouth corners
Look closely ever so slight
Work-booted foot taps
To keep time

Alchemy

Worship is innate
Something—
A river or the sun
To ascribe power
That might be out of reach
Or not
Alchemists measured
movements of the stars
Looked to the earth
For miracles
Recognize outside influences
Humble willing to listen
Quietly sit silent
Wait for the inter-ear
To respond to celestial whispers
Shoot like lightning
Through nerves veins and vessels
Carry the stuff of stories
Race along all the contours
Of the brain
To be filtered and processed
Made ready to leap from lips
Or flow from fingers
Scratched on paper
Physical evidence
Art unassailable
By outside ignorance
Or apathy
High art prayers to honor
Not found in white noise
Or sucked into black holes
To never escape
But crushed to nothing
Sifted like sand in an hourglass

Rematerialized and shot
From a white hole
Reshaped to unorganized mass
Pushed into form
Foundation blocks to build on
Once again and again and yet again

When I Heard the Learn'd Astronomer (Part Two)

Till rising and gliding out I wander'd off by myself
—Walt Whitman

While Whitman stares out the window
Pondering the constellations
Looking for Orion
The North Star Big Dipper
His mind like a light sail
Transcends speeding through
The universe pushed by sunlight

Not hampered by lectures ancient and dry
Captivated by natural magic
Black night sky
Alive with streaking stars
Heavenly lights by the millions
Planets Venus Mars the Moon

What he learned
All would do well to learn
Look see observe
Electrified by miracles
Eclipse of the Sun and Moon
"In mystical moist night air"
Let minds be carried away

Breakfast with Shelby Foote at Snappy Service

He said the Civil War
had two geniuses
Abraham Lincoln and Nathan Bedford Forest
Half of what he said was rejected
As he spoke
General Forest's granddaughter's
face flashed red
back board straight
fiery eyes
Radiated anger and insult
Her frosted response
"Well sir, we don't think much of Mr. Lincoln in this house"
This unrecorded bit of history
Delivered matter of fact
Over bacon and eggs buttered toast
And coffee
Diamond prisms flashed from
River blue eyes
Leaning back in the chair
Smile pushed through a gray beard
He asked for a refill
And packed his pipe with tobacco.

By Candlelight

By candlelight a pencil
scratches across rough paper
last lines before
"going over the top"

Air flooded with anticipation
and fear
the rattle of kit as soldiers
lift packs rifles loaded

Boys white with fear
tear streaked cheeks
some hide behind
profanity and bravado
eyes that can't hide concern

Shouts of sergeants
platoons line up
tin helmets give a false
sense of security

Orders filter down from generals
away from the front
secure in requisitioned villas
and hotels

They play a game of attrition
with young lives when
sending faceless boys to die
in rat filled trenches

By bullets bombs gas
neck-deep mud
In "No Man's Land"

Scarface

Capone lays with the dead
At 25 a Chicago power house
Strong and cold ruthless and angry
As the wind off Lake Michigan
Son of the old code

He ruled the underworld
By bullet and blood
One Valentine's Day
He sent lead arrows to 7 men
Delivered mechanically
By Mr. Thompson's machine gun

Cheating on taxes
Not murder sent him to Alcatraz
4 years with the Bird Man
and Machine Gun Kelly

Mind deranged by syphilis
Released from the Rock
To seven years of Florida sun
Left with a child's mind

He Fell for the Rest of His Life

The margin of error remaining satisfyingly narrow
—Harold Drasdo

Loneliest of places
Sharp end of a climbing rope
Climber leaves the horizontal
Steps into the vertical
Before vision becomes tunneled
Immediate microscopic
Sets a line—places of purchase
Each upward move
And several ahead planned
Chess master
Exactness economy
Strength banked for the crux

Leaves the ground
Dances from small hold
To even smaller
Tendons stretch to near breaking
Lactic acid eats muscle
Mind the master of ascent
Labors to focus
Protect every six feet
Second chance to ground fall
All's fair
Rock horn chock stone natural or artificial
Lug or machine nuts
Strung with rope
Forged iron finger nail thin
Soft aluminum mashies
Perfected by experience
Learn rules then break them
Hubris vanity ego
Invincible

Risk unclearly calculated
Extends the bet
Clouds psyche with false confidence
Pushes past the edge
Second of clarity
Vision blurred by gravity
Roar of wind ears explode
Eyes water
Emotions freeze
A thousand thoughts
End in sudden solitude
Darkness overtakes light

Old Ghosts

Quiet street
Old ghosts meet
Hollow eyes
Transfixed vision in reverse
Grief stricken sorrow
Vomiting dead youth
One day sixty thousand
And more died
In mindless slaughter
The Butcher* architect of defeat
Military autocrats
Plot in luxury well back
A war of attrition
Army on its back foot
Sea of churned earth
The blood of innocence
Frozen by fear
Tear-stained faces
Press against stone lined trench walls
Swallowing back the acid of doubt
Intimate reality—haunted
Wagner's Chorus of the Gods

*Field Marshall Lord Haig: He was nicknamed "Butcher Haig" for the two million British casualties endured under his command. The Canadian War Museum comments, "His epic but costly offensives at the Somme (1916) and Passchendaele (1917) have become nearly synonymous with the carnage and futility of First World War battles."

A Stick of Gum

—For Doug Rowe

The same hand that can write a beautiful poem,
can knock you out with one punch—that's Poetic Justice.
— "Irish" Wayne Kelly

A stick of gum started it
Ended with a broken jaw
Black eye lasted year
He gave her gum
Flavor no matter

Act of giving mattered
To give my girl gum
She wasn't really mine
We weren't going steady
Just Friday night visits
Sit in her front room
Look out the window at nothing
I'd sneak my arm around her shoulder
Holding her hand
As far as things went

No other boys hung about
She liked me coming round
Made her my girl
That kid with the gum
Was trespassing—a challenge

Church yard was off school grounds
Madison Square Garden of Mound Fort
It's the first punch that most matters
Something yet to learn
Shed my coat and turned

Hit hard jaw snapped
Punched again same place
Not much fight left
Forgot where I was

Walked home alone trying to remember
Not much came to me
Playground rules I was vanquished
Warned off

For a year my defeat
Showed when I washed my face combed my hair
Passed by a store window
Lost love lost pride
Embarrassment open for all to see

Tonight in Sun Valley

Tonight in Sun Valley
Mathew Arnold passed through
Dropped in from 1851
Still going on about the Beach
His words put to music
Dissonant notes spring from
Violin viola cello harsh
Like crashing waves of the Channel
Across and through the amphitheater
Releasing two-hundred-year old emotion
To challenge the human heart
Through ears and eyes
Past and present
An infinity of emotion
Conflicting notes
Explode over the audience
Lost on no one
Seeping through every pore
To remote recess
Heart and lungs
Bowels
Circulates in veins
Carried in and out
By both red and white cells
Senses fire nerves explode
A wrestling match between poetry
And music.

A Conversation with God

Windows and mirrors shatter
Light bulbs explode
Voices echo from nowhere
A kind of revelation
Nothing specific but profound
Seeps through cedar shingles
Gray with age
Cracked and wrinkled
Isolation and depression
Anxiety and reflection
Meditation and prayer
Anger and sorrow
Tears and laughter
Fair play and cheaters

Past and present
Reality and fantasy
Weakness and strength
Fear and bravery
Sacrifice and service
Move forward or stand pat
Learn from mistakes
Stopping and starting
Discretion and valor
Beauty and simplicity?

Cobbler

He has bequeathed his nation a body of imperishable verse from which Americans will forever gain joy and understanding. He saw poetry as the means of saving power from itself. When power leads man towards arrogance, poetry reminds him of his limitations. When power narrows the areas of man's concern, poetry reminds him of the richness and diversity of his existence. When power corrupts, poetry cleanses.
—President John F. Kennedy

Today I read about Robert Frost
Said he was searching
Often his dark meditations
Run like spilt ink
Across the geography of New England

Though born in San Francisco
After Dartmouth & Harvard
He taught cobbled edited
Tried farming

In England wrote poetry
Met Brooks Graves & Taylor
Ezra Pound rescued his words
Like he did Elliot's
Left America failed farmer
Returned poet

A star + 2 books
Others rolling around
In his head gestating
Waiting for the right moment
To appear on stiff foolscap
Word-pictures in blue and black

Prizes for his poems
Fell like ripe apples
Gold medals 4 Pulitzers

Congress willing to accept
Even his darkest words
Snarling & rattling

Uncomfortable words
Good fences make good neighbors
Boys in birch trees
Hired men horses in deep winter
Ants & tramps
Tilling soil chopping wood
Fire & ice love & hate sorrow & pain

Time alive like new crops
Death destroying innocence
Words & blood smell of oil
Mountain ranges follow the sun
Endlessly winding west
Another day dies
Takes everything that matters

Blake & Hopkins brothers of another time
Industry & semi-revolution
Mind stretching contradictions
Caves & Allegories
Earth bleared smeared
Satanic mills drawing life
From men's souls

Thawing wind tosses
Pages like leaves
Rhymes scattered not lost
Thoughts want further thinking
Paths want walking
Spirit in wildness & apple orchards

Dance

From hill top
Waves float silent
Over deep blue
Roar as they crash
Against sand rock
Lost to distance

Pen dipped rich indigo
Flows magically on cloud-white linen
Paints vivid images
Sing dance
Music with no notes

Motion rhythmic metered
Gladness sorrow sneaks
Down dark cobbled alleys
Beautiful breaks soars
Teases moon stars
Angels eternity

DNA

Did he who made the lamb make thee…
—William Blake

Nature, red in tooth and claw...
—Alfred, Lord Tennyson

Patterson hunted Savo Lions
Ghost and Darkness
Worked through thorny perimeters
Past bonfires and warders
Wander into tents
A tag team
Drag men away
Lions don't hunt in pairs

Vasconcelos-Calderon's boar hunters
Themselves superior killing machines
Equipped with rifle and reason
Murder indiscriminately
Senseless brutes
Evolutionary tables turned
Hunters became hunted
Only fit survive

Tigers don't hunt humans
Not in their DNA
Man-Eater of Champawat
Hunted Himalayan foothills
Ten years eluded
Assassins bounty hunter
Even Gurkha soldiers
Four hundred killed
Corbett ended it
"Desperate times require desperate measures"

Dreamer of Dreams

My father had much in common
With Old Testament prophets
A dreamer of dreams
Once at breakfast
More sedate reflective
In hushed tone he told of a dream

He spoke as if alone
As if I hadn't been born
My mother a non-entity
He was in New York
Winter the city under snow
Quite devoid of life

He stood atop a tall building
Amidst other tall buildings
More building across the way
A river between the buildings
Like black asphalt

Skyward several planes in formation
Aligned for landing
The planes within easy reach
He nearly touched them
Stared inside the cockpit
Recognized the pilots
First his father nodded smiled
Frantically warning of river
Not safe
Helpless it hit water broke apart
Slipped under

Next plane neared
Its pilot Bob Wright
Continued his descent
Hit the water disappeared
Third plane came
Like looking in a mirror
He saw himself
Lost like the others

My father was fearless
He rehearsed his dream
Unnerved unsteady pale
Confused waiting for a response
He called it a premonition
A warning a revelation

His father died on Christmas Day
Bob Wright was next
Buried beneath December snow

Faces were strained
Eyes glassy with worry
Dad had glimpsed the future
Resigned to his dream
Just two days after Bob
Dad died on New Year's Eve
Shortly before midnight

Have You Thought About Writing

Have you thought about writing about Scotland
  the Isle of Skye
  the Black Cuillin
  Sgurr Alistair
  the Great Stone Shute

About how hardness & sharp edges of gabbro
  how it rips clothes & tears skin
  crushes bone & severs tendon and sinew

About the far Scot north & Atlantic storms
  freezing winds & being alone
  feeling lost & feeling pain

About life & death
  love & responsibility
  fear & resolution

About the end from the beginning
  instinct & knowledge
  experience & consequences
  rationalization & justification
  joy & sorrow

About broken bones & torn muscle
  surgery & scars
  worn joints & replacements
  surgeons & therapists
  crutches & canes
  braces & prosthetics

About isolation & depression
        anxiety & reflection
        meditation & prayer
        anger & sorrow
        tears & laughter

About fair play & cheaters
        past & present
        reality & fantasy
        weakness & strength
        fear & bravery
        sacrifice & service

About moving forward
        or standing pat
        learning from
        the mistakes of other
        or from your own
        stopping & starting
        discretion & valor
        beauty & simplicity

About "taking the road less traveled,"
        & finally acceptance

He Loved Lightning

For Nolan Kohler

Those who dance are considered mad
By those who cannot hear the music.
                    —Friedrich Nietzsche

He loved lightning
Thunder a song
Each flash divine
Clap and rumble
Shook his inner foundation
Fearless in heavy weather
He faced blackness
A prophet awaiting God's voice
Standing in strong winds
He'd say "did you see that"
Comfort meaningless
Fire of spirit his warmth
Simple guileless pure
Lost in simple metaphysics
Wonders of heaven unexplained
Pillar of fire burning bush
Arrows shot by gods or angels
Music only he can hear

One Million Ghosts and More

Hide in stairwells alley ways
    Off the path beaten uneven
Where brownstone or brick walls
    Turn to gray cement then slide
Into the ground occasionally a dim light
    Creeps out from ground-level windows
So dirty yellow light is forced
    To make itself known to do what light does

Windows witness to decades centuries
    Of human footfalls crape sole work boots
Sleek Italian calf skins
    Young girls out for the night stumble
Along the uneven brick roads
    Spike heels threatened by joints missing mortar
Lurk hungry to snap ankles

Dead end closed in by hard walls
    That disappear in the night sky
Lonely terrifying silence
    Broken by the cry of a hungry child
Harsh words between man and wife
    Light yellow squares dot giant blackness
Opaque and out of reach

Garbage cans rattle feral cats after big city rats
    Rats and the homeless dig for dinner
In blue dumpsters full of human refuse
    Rotten lettuce potatoes spoiled meat
Bones stripped clean by butcher's knife
    And ugly yellow rat's teeth helped along
By writhing white maggots

Clouds reflect mysterious moon shadows
Casts down dim silver light
Seeps into every hiding place
Chases away the unknown
The sun warm bright answers
An invitation to a new day

Playthings of Un-Earthly Visitors

In the hills of north Cumbria
Is a quiet pasture slightly mounded
Which at its high point
(If one looks south
The Vale of St. John
Cuts its way
Between the rounded shoulders
Of Cloughs Head and Ravens Crag
Past the little church on the east
And Thirlmere to the west)
Is a circle of standing stones
Smaller, but much older
Than its infinitely more famous cousin in the South
Where great pillars of Bluestone
Rise magically from the plain
In both cases some think them to be
Druid Temples
Or calendars of when to sow and reap
Or the playthings of un-earthly visitors
How did Welsh stone come to stand in Salisbury
And Castlerigg to be in Keswick

Resurrected by the Dead

If the thunder don't get ya' the lighting will.
—Jerry Garcia

I do crazy things sometimes
Back when possessing a joint
Meant jail
Ate one for a friend

Cruising Washington Avenue
Going nowhere
CCR eight track
Arguing politics

Missed yellow ran red
Flashing red lights
Cracked night sky
Terror police state
Chernobyl-like meltdown

Stopped by a tire store
"Where you boys been"
"What's your destination"
"Been drinking—its late"

Terrified sober
Tremors wide eyes
Near miss
Political debate
No conclusion

"Way leads on to way"
School work families
Time memories
Topography separation

Miracle accident fate
Pathways converge
Align past with future
Time swirls blue ink in water
Mysterious beautiful unexpected
Dream-like revelatory transcendent

Earth's spin
Diverse places
Adolescences adulthood
Business law Iowa
Geography time distance
Dreams adventures dimmed
Restricted courage mitigated
Exaggerated relative

Time explodes
Free speech environment civil rights
Race gender religion
Democrats Republicans
Rock n roll

Woodstock Monterey Big Sir Altamont
Dylan Byrds Beatles Joni Mitchell
CSN&Y the Stones, Booker T
Sly Stone Richie Havens Donovan
Los Lobos Kris Kristofferson PP&M

Past slammed present
By accident
Stars never align so
Salt Palace August 12, 1981

Music electricity anticipation
Hippies Dead-Heads Mormons
Doctors lawyers heathens
Uncle John's Band Dire Wolf Truckin'

Instantly magical time Place
Accident happenstance strange
Idealistic excited liberated
Friendship after ten years
Resurrected by the Dead

Voluntary Isolation

For The Brothers of Our Lady of the Holy Trinity, Huntsville, Utah

If you have built castles in the air, your work need not be lost; that is where they should be. Now put the foundations under them.

—Henry David Thoreau

To the top of the high arched ceiling
Language of God
Is carried aloft on the breath
Of a scant choir they exhale chants
Drawn back as lungs cry for air
Reloaded voices send forth
Collective memory of a thousand monks
Committed to God
Labor in farm fields
Like the first parents
Eat by the sweat of their brows
Eschew the material
To seek the spiritual
Life absent of offence

Staff of Life

Food
Gritts
Pancakes
Crepesda
Lasagna
Hot dogs
Escargot
Lemberg
Horse radish
Tongue
Curry
Sesame seeds
Saffron
Chili
Sea salt
Calzone
Fried fish
Green onions
Chestnuts
Apricots
Olives
Pemican
Rice
Rhubarb
Squash
Squid
Bologna
Shepherd's pie
Cupcakes
Potatoes
Parsnips
Pickled cauliflower
Calamari
Black olives

Broccoli
Rutabagas
Rolled oats
Brisket
Brussel sprouts

We All Have Stories

We all have stories
Many not unlike that of *Sophie's
That need be told
To establish a story
Or set the story straight
To fix dates of birth or death
To set the stage
Where it should be staged
The right place
For the story
It may not be tragic
Or difficult
Destructive and dark destroy sanity
Cause eyes to fade
To turn blue eyes gray
And dried up
No tears left
After a lifetime of sorrow
Mouth frozen in a frown
Slumped shoulders bowed back
Feet so heavy to walk
Beyond a shuffle impossible
Weighted in psychological chains
Like Dicken's Marley
Aching to reach the grave
Not to seek salvation
Only to hide
Enveloped in darkness.

Sophie's Choice by William Styron

Something

Worship is innate
Something—
A river or the sun
To ascribe power
That might be out of reach
Or not
Alchemists measured
movements of the stars
Looked to the earth
For miracles
Recognize outside influences
Humble willing to listen
Quietly sit silent
Wait for the inter-ear
To respond to celestial whispers
Shoot like lightening
Through nerves veins and vessels
Carry the stuff of stories
Race along all the contoured
Of the brain
To be filtered and processed
Made ready to leap from lips
Or flow from fingers
Scratched on paper
Physical evidence
Art unassailable
By outside ignorance
Or apathy
High art prayers to honor
Not found in white noise
Or sucked into black holes
To never escape
But crushed to nothing
Sifted like sand in an hourglass

Caves

I was once
Attracted to caves
Mystery in blackness
Holes in earth
Home to snakes spiders
Other things
Scent pleasant decay
Fill nostrils mouths
Tastes of mold
Cool dampness draws
Inky darkness's sirens call
Overwhelming silence
Broken with stumbling footfall
Loose rock spider webs
Other shenanigans
Twisted ankles bumped heads
Clumsy voices explode silence

In the Churchyard of St. Thomas the Apostle

The paths of glory lead but to the grave.
—Thomas Gray

Some call me Electra
But my name is Sylvia
Cold Yorkshire ground
Holds my bones
Carried north from London
Still smelling of gas
The oven smaller
Than those used by the Germans
But just as deadly

I empathize with Jews
Packed in cattle cars
Taken from their homes
To the camps
With the promise
That work will set them free
In my case it was art

Daddy daddy
Panzer-man
Cleft chin
Aryan eye
Champion of biology and eugenics
Swastika arm raised in a Hitler salute
Finger nails like Nazi bayonets
Scrape death across Ivy League blackboards

Star crossed at Cambridge
Ted seven years your name was mine too
We spoke through poetry
Yet my despair
Like "An owl's talons clenching my heart"
Was inescapable except

After these many years
They still come with hammer and chisel
To free me
Attacking your name
Leaving a scar on my marble stone
Like the one on my cheek
My "marble heavy" badge of honor
Key to eternity

Outside Ettersberg

Inside the gates
Of Buchenwald
A blacked stump
Is all that remains
Of Goethe's Oak

Branches that once
Cast welcome shade
A symbol of art and honor
A place for poets

It stood at the center
Of the camp
It's loveliness and spirit tarnished
It's reverence stained
Roots drenched with lost innocence

Cries of the tortured
Bodies and spirits
Humiliated by skulled and crossboned
Supermen in jackboots
Willingly malignant

A haven desecrated
Turned pillory and gallows
Branches bent by bodies hanged
Foreshadowed gas showers
Ovens to reduce humans
To smoke and ashes

Wagnerian marches
Nietzschean myth
Clicking heals and Heil Hitlers
Drown memory of poetry and music
Over-soul turned victim
Nature moans

Ariel bombs
Turn Goethe's Oak to ash and smoke
To a blackened stump
Emblem of numberless people
Cremated to hide atrocities

At the Cross-Roads

After all, we had chosen to cast our lot among the hills.
—Thomas Firbank

For three hundred years
The Pen-Y-Gwyrd Hotel
Has stood at the cross-roads
From Capel Curig to Pen-Y-Pass
With Snowdon's great bulk to the west
And Tryfan and the Glyders to the east.

In autumn, when days grow short
And mist hides the mountaintops
Grey fingers claw
Down the crags
Across winter-killed moors
That holds tenaciously to the warmth
Of faded day-light reflected
In white-paned windows
While the creeper that grows
On the aged granite walls blazes fiery-red
A prophesy of long, dark winter days.

September September 1964

I grew up in Ogden, Utah
Wild West town
Hard to imagine
Hearing gun shots
Ring out on Chester Street
Once a peach orchard small farms
Morphed to American middle class

Mostly old people
Neat bungalows and set ways
Guns going off
Screams and broken glass
Profanity most base
As if graves were opening
The dead rose

True story
There were gun shots
Bad language broken windows
Tempered glass picture window
Shattered by a woman's body
And landing against the porch railing
Then again sound shattered

She shot her husband
In the stomach
Seeing someone hit by a .38 slug
Still able to retaliate
To throw his wife
Through plate glass
No one died

She was on her feet only bruises
Able at the top of her lungs
Spit out words I'd never heard before
Bullet missed his vital parts
Pasted through one ample love handle
Blood and pain
Accounted for additional vulgarities
Lasting until the police and ambulance arrived

This racket terribly inconvenient
Gillette Friday Night Fights
Playing on our new Zenith black and white
That only weeks earlier
Replaced an old transatlantic radio
The fights was a religious event at our house
A catechism of sorts
Sacrament of buttered popcorn cold Coke

Before the TV
My dad and his dad
Sat on chair's edge
Throwing punches at imaginary opponents
Jimmy Powers did the blow by blow
Focused concentration until final bell
Interruption as not tolerated—no excuse
Even by gun shots
Or a woman flying through plate glass
Regardless how out of the ordinary

Fights were more than athletics
A sacred social commentary
Inside the ropes everyone is equal
No color barriers
Religion didn't matter

Equal pay for a winner regardless
Golden Age of manly combat
Bonding time for father and son

Reached its pinnacle with
Kid Gavilan
Benny (Kid) Paret
Carmine Basilio
Gene and Don Fullmer
Florentino Fernandez
Nino Benenutti
Emile Griffith
Friday nights revered as the 12 Apostles
Interruption blasphemy

Morbid curiosity adrenaline
Got the best of us
Drawing dad's dad and me
Out on the porch
Dad was in the street
Collected the gun called for a towel
To staunch blood coursing
From wounded love handle
Stood silent just whispers
Until relieved by the police

This landmark disturbance
Cast a pall on the neighborhood
That for some lasted a lifetime
Foreshadowed the end
Of an American tradition
Don Fullmer's loss to Dick Tiger
On 9/11/1964 in Cleveland
KOed The Friday Night Fights

9/11 inauspicious date synonymous
With another American tragedy
Thirty-seven years later to the day

Knee Deep Snow New Year's Eve, 1966

Dad—50 years dead

To Everything (Turn, Turn, Turn)
There is a season (Turn, Turn, Turn)
And a time to every purpose, under Heaven
　　　　　　　　　　—Pete Seeger

A week ago, Christmas
at his father's grave
I heard him say
"that ground looks so cold,
I hope when I go it's warm"

Above the cemetery
gray-black clouds cast
shadows over
Lake Bonneville's terraces
scraped
across the west face
of the Wasatch
Nature's mysteries secrets
stories scribbled in dirt, rock, & bones
hide in
Cold deep snow

To the west
gray-white alkali flats
a thousand years just right of time's meridian
Scoured scraped stretched
to nothing
winds carry the songs
of the dead
stir imagination

We stand
feet in two centuries
one where it's possible to harvest organs
take a heart from one
put in another
walk on the moon
climb highest mountains,
drop into black bottomless waters
yet hold to
customs of arcane myth superstition
seeks to extend life
physicians dance with the shadows of
Paracelsus, Agrippa & Albertus Magnus
wrestle to subdue death's frosty grip
search secrets lost to
the dark side of mortality
The way of all flesh
leads to the grave

Science
life a gamble
a flip of a coin
what of Pascal's wager
heads wins
tails nothing

"The greatest snow on earth"
continues to blanket the Wasatch mountains
freezes on unplowed roads
winter slow magical
carpet of white
silent reflector of ambient light

Orion lost in ink-black skies
short frozen days
a conjuring time
of paradox joy & sorrow

Just after the New Year
a plea unheard
It's his turn
buried against his will
in a cold hole
snow, knee deep
a still-life out of Dickens.

Requiem

Anglesey's west coast
Angry Atlantic
Blasts against battered rock faces
Of Puffin Island
Moss holds tenaciously
Against salty attack

Invisible just below the surface
Sharks prowl next to rock
On alert for birds
That approach the very edge
Of the black rock
Tempt those
Many-toothed monsters
Wait watching hubcap eyes
Single-minded for a Puffin's errant step
Whose careless ends
A single symbiotic snap
Feathers and bone disappear
Fast as lightning

Secondary Sources

This came second hand
A voice echoes repeatedly
As from heaven
Or the serpent

Light to dark & back
Advantage easily shifted
Room for interpretation
Fails in accuracy & control

Life ambiguous forth & back
Civil boundaries right angles
Restrict freedom

Latitude is dangerous
Every twelve hours
Darkness overtakes light
Limits far clear vision

In shadows things unhinge
Are not as they appear
Right & wrong bend Nature
Twist speculation & half truths

Simplicity of Eden
Replaced thorns & thistles
Clear water cool air
Carry poison

Lost vigilance
Speeds the takeover
Blurred minds clouded eyes
Fail to see
Dark destruction's blitz

Springtime in Hawkshead

Regular seasons
Cold chased away
Days grow longer
Darkness is overtaken
Brown earth turns green
Life in hibernation awakes
Soiled white of late winter melts
Little rivulets sneak off
Gives way to earth's patchwork of wild flowers
Stiff limbs stretch become fluid
Little creatures venture from winter rest
Green fifty shades cover hills
Lift steeply from cobalt waters
Dot quiet valleys sparkle like emeralds
As sun creeps from behind mountains
Beams break through rain clouds
Makes the morning dewdrops prisms
Rainbow colors jump about
In celebration.

The Hope of the Sun

And through the last lights off the black West went
                              —Gerard Manley Hopkins

The sign said
the best places to visit
it must refer to places near by
within walking distance
Who could make such a declaration?

Surely a local
someone who knows each street
shortcuts learned while young.

The hope of the Sun never sets
even as the light goes dark
dropping over earth's edge.

Hope's golden rays continue to shine on other side
for those who saw both come and go yesterday.
As you do now
darkness chases away things to hope for
yet joy springs with the first dim light from the east.

Joy will not be denied
it pushes up through
the dust and ashes of yesterday.

When the World Ends

When the world ends
will it be overrun by tanks
like Armadillos
the sting of a Manticore's
Scorpion tail
Or ancient creatures resurrected
from test tubes
Possibly pregnant clouds
drift silently
dropping poison
makes snow sparkle
waters turn deadly black
Earth suffocated because
forests cut clear
by greed
What about those
who come after us

Elegy: For a Sparrow

Who trusted God was love indeed
And love Creation's final law
Tho' Nature, red in tooth and claw
With ravine, shriek'd against his creed
                    —Alfred Lord Tennyson

On the scraggly apricot branch
A drama plays out
For any who will
To watch
Flat steely sky
A sparrow
Gray-brown feathers
Pulled tight against
Late-day winter cold
The plot common
A metaphor over-used

Tiny heart metronome
In its fragile feathered chest
Beats faint rhythm
A funeral dirge
Deep and slow
The spare protagonist
Remains in character
Like a "camp survivor"
Holds tenaciously the branch
Reconciled to winter's insult
Stage lights dim
Its silhouette remains
Frozen in place
Until darkness closes the curtain.

What Said the Thunder...

—T. S. Eliot

Lightening shatters cobalt sky
Jagged electricity charges to earth
As if an angry Zeus
Is visiting destruction
On all living
The blinding flash
Followed by a crack of thunder
Children count the time
One-one hundred
Two-one hundred
Three-one hundred
An attempt to judge
If they should be scared

When my dad was a boy
By the kitchen sink
A laser flash shot from the black clouds
Blowing in from the southwest
Struck the vent pipe
Outside the window
Shattered glass showered daggers throughout the room
On the floor
Covered and cut
He was stupid for a while
Disoriented and lost

The air smelled of ozone
Scent of Satan
A black scar
Followed the pipe into the ground
Maybe clear to Hell
Or it might have bounced back to the clouds
To recharge and strike again

White Buffalo

I have taught one doctrine, namely, the infinitude of private man.
                                        —Ralph Waldo Emerson

*He was ten. But it had already begun, long before that day when at last he
wrote his age in two figures and he saw for the first time the camp where his
father and Major de Spain and old General Compson and the others spent
two weeks each November and two weeks again each June. He had already
inherited then, without ever having seen it, the tremendous bear with one
trap-ruined foot which, in an area almost a hundred miles deep, had earned
itself a name, a definite designation like a living man.*
                                        —William Faulkner

It was real—I swear
Standing alone
Silhouetted in afternoon sun
On a rise overlooking a
Sea of golden prairie grass
Dream-like—noble
One in ten-million
Sacred to the Cheyenne Flathead
Oglala Lakota Arapaho
Purity mind spirit body
Hope unity good times
Oneness with all living
Walking prayer—meditation
Renewal of spirit
Reflection of God's love
Clear to holy men and children
I saw it as a boy
Outside Hardin, Montana's
Old curio shop
My drum and tomahawk in hand
Separate reality
To a child
Real tangible natural

White Caps at Lincoln City

For Mark and Linda

White caps crash
On sand black rock
Blue-green Pacific water
Blends slate grey sky

Mysterious flat light conjures
Lost ships ghosts of sailors
Imagination floats massed schooners
North and San Juans

Orcas rise dance in waters off Anacortes
Totems stand sentinel
Peer through fog banks
That slip in and out of costal spruce forests

Silence broken
Gulls screech dart
After dead fish bread crumbs
Like the ocean noisy eternal

About the Author

Mikel Vause holds a PhD from Bowling Green University. He is the author of numerous articles, poems, and short stories and is the editor of six books. His poetry collections are: *I knew It would Come to This; A Mountain Touched by Fire; At the Edge of Things; Looking for the Old Crown; The Scent of Juniper; and A Home to Strange Animals.* In 2016 he was a Pushcart Prize nominee for his poem "What said the Thunder."

www.ingramcontent.com/pod-product-compliance
Lightning Source LLC
Chambersburg PA
CBHW031150090426
42738CB00008B/1281